REUSE IT!
MARLA CONN
Rourke Educational Media
A Division of Carson Dellosa Education
I0892848

Photo Glossary

bottle

box

can

jar

roll

tire

High Frequency Words:

- can
- is
- it
- not
- reuse
- this
- trash
- we

This **roll** is not trash.

We can reuse it.

This **jar** is not trash.

We can reuse it.

This **can** is not trash.

We can reuse it.

This **tire** is not trash.

We can reuse it.

This **bottle** is not trash.

We can reuse it.

This **box** is not trash.

We can reuse it.

Activity

1. Go back and read the story with a partner.
2. Discuss the objects in the story that can be reused. Give examples of how you use and reuse these things.
3. Discuss different ways that you can reuse the items in the pictures below.

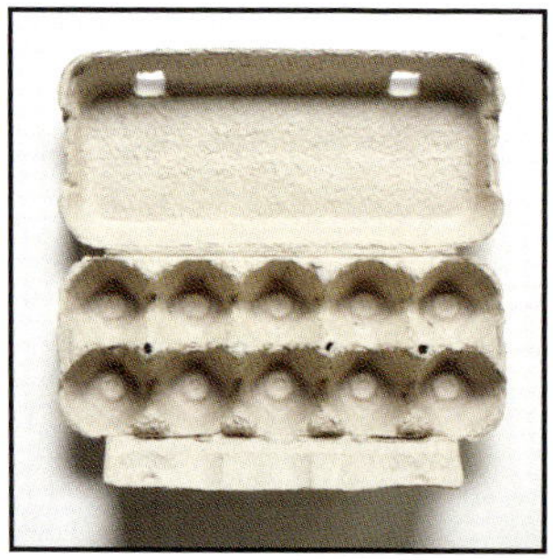

4. Create a poster that tells people in your school community to reuse and recycle.